Garry Chapman

eXtreme SPORTS

STREETS

WARNING:

Extreme sports can be very dangerous. Mishaps can result in death or serious injury. Seek expert advice before attempting any of the stunts you read about in this book.

This book is for Ian, Theresa, Emma and Sarah Liddle.

This edition first published in 2002 in the United States of America by Chelsea House Publishers, a subsidiary of Haights Cross Communications.

Reprinted 2002

Chelsea House Publishers
1974 Sproul Road, Suite 400
Broomall, PA 19008-0914

The Chelsea House world wide web address is www.chelseahouse.com

Library of Congress Cataloging-in-Publication Data Applied for.

ISBN 0-7910-6612-6

First published in 2001 by
Macmillan Education Australia Pty Ltd
627 Chapel Street, South Yarra, Australia, 3141

Copyright © Garry Chapman 2001

Edited by Renée Otmar, Otmar Miller Consultancy Pty Ltd
Text design by if design
Cover design by if design
Printed in China

Acknowledgements

The author and the publisher are grateful to the following for permission to reproduce copyright material:

Cover photo: BMX rider courtesy of Sport. The Library/Lutz Bongarts.

AAP Image, pp. 12–13 (insert); Allsport/Jamie Squire, p. 11; Austral/Rex, pp. 6–7; Image Bank/
A.T. Willett, p. 25 (insert); PhotoDisc, pp. 5, 17, 20–21, 30; Sport. The Library, pp. 9, 22 (insert); Sport. The Library/Chris Elfes, p. 4; Sport. The Library/Darren England, pp. 12–13, 15; Sport. The Library/Ian Kenins, p. 10; Sport. The Library/Lutz Bongarts, pp. 22–23; Sport. The Library/Mao Presse, p. 18; Sport. The Library/Peter Schatz, p. 27; Sport. The Library/Presse Sports, p. 8; Sport. The Library/Scott Needham, p. 14; Sporting Images, p. 16; Sporting Images/Andrew Shield, pp. 24–25; Sporting Images/Duane Hart, pp. 26, 28 (bottom), 28–29; Stock Photos/Masterfile/Peter Griffith, p. 19.

While every care has been taken to trace and acknowledge copyright the publishers tender their apologies for any accidental infringement where copyright has proved untraceable.

DISCLAIMER
The extreme sports described in this book are potentially dangerous, and can result in death or serious injury if attempted by inexperienced persons. The author and the publishers wish to advise readers that they take no responsibility for any mishaps that may occur as the result of persons attempting to perform the activities described in this book.

Contents

Street sport action at the Bondi Beach Skate Park, Sydney

Traditional pastimes

For hundreds of years, the broad streets, narrow lanes and open public spaces of cities, towns and villages have been the favorite playgrounds of the people who live in the neighborhood. It was not unusual to see a group of children kicking a ball in a deserted street, playing hopscotch on a pavement, or hide and seek in a park.

THE ELEMENT OF DANGER

Some of these traditional street pastimes even had an element of danger. Children dared each other to see how high they could climb up trees. Others nailed blocks of wood to long poles and tried walking on stilts, with mixed success. Billycart races down steep hills often resulted in cuts and bruises for their daredevil riders.

Organized sports evolve

Over time, new sports for townspeople evolved. Some of these sports became so popular that clubs and associations were formed. The sporting clubs and associations built specialized venues and held regular competitions. Athletics, tennis, baseball, cricket and various codes of football are examples of such sports.

SPEED, WHEELS AND A SLOPED SURFACE

These organized sports, however, do not appeal to everyone. Many people still prefer to take part in street activities that allow them to set their own limits, take a few risks and experience the thrill of adrenaline pumping through their bodies. The combination of speed, wheels and a sloped surface has as much appeal to many people today as it had to billycart riders so many years ago. A new generation of street sports enthusiasts even take their sporting action to extreme lengths.

Skate park action

Many people prefer to join their friends for a bit of skating fun at a local venue. There might be a **skate park** nearby, complete with ramps, bowls and **transitions** specially constructed for use by skateboarders. If a skate park is not available, you can generally make do with an empty carpark, a vacant block or almost any other public place that features stairs, handrails and lots of concrete. Skateboarding is one of the most adrenaline-pumping action sports imaginable.

TAKING STREET SPORTS TO EXTREMES

GLOSSARY

skate park – a community area featuring a halfpipe, bowls, ramps and other obstacles used by street sports enthusiasts

transitions – the curved walls that join the horizontal plane to the vert wall on a ramp or halfpipe

tricks – also known as stunts; the movements performed in street sports that include airs, grinds, slides, grabs, spins and flips

Xtreme Fact

Skate parks often schedule separate sessions for BMX bikers and skaters. There are now also many indoor skate parks, often located in former warehouse buildings.

Skateboarding culture

Skateboarding appeals to people for many reasons:

- ☞ **you do not need a lot of equipment**
- ☞ **you can do it on your own or in a group**
- ☞ **you can start with few skills and gradually extend your limits**
- ☞ **you can do it almost anywhere.**

A culture has grown up around skateboarding. Skateboarding has its own 'language', its own fashions and brand names, its own music and its own heroes. In the skateboarding culture, every new trick mastered earns the respect of other skateboarders.

Inline skaters

Aggressive inline skaters have also taken their sport to the streets. This sport shares many similarities with skateboarding. Inline skaters also like to hang out at skate parks and other places where they can jump, slide, grind and generally have a good time.

BMX options

BMX riders have found a home in the cities. Dirt courses, featuring sharp corners and spectacular jumps, provide entertainment for those who love the thrills and spills of racing. Skate parks also cater for those who prefer to perform **tricks** with their bikes.

High-speed street luge

A few very daring extreme sports enthusiasts take up street luge. This fast action sport is not for the faint-hearted. It involves lying flat on your back, just inches above the ground, and hurtling downhill at speeds of greater than 100 kilometers (62 miles) per hour. Street lugers understand fear very well — they just do not show it!

Street sports

City and town sports have been redefined on the streets. If it involves jumping, spinning, flipping or just going really fast, you will probably find it happening in our streets and parks.

Street Sports Venues

Sidewalk surfing

Extreme street sports started in California in the United States of America. The first skateboard was produced there in 1958. A surf shop owner began mounting boards onto sets of wheels specially produced by the Chicago Roller Skate Company. The initial craze was known as 'sidewalk surfing'. By the early 1960s, it had spread to the surfing community, who likened it to the sensation felt when riding a wave.

Skate parks become popular

Interest in skateboarding grew rapidly in the mid-1970s. Local communities across the United States built skate parks to provide recreational facilities for young people. Soon there were hundreds across the country.

A setback for skateboarding

As more and more skaters began to use the skate parks, the number of skateboard-related injuries grew. Fearing that people might sue their local councils for negligence, the insurance companies raised their fees. Many local authorities could no longer afford to pay the insurance fees, so they banned skateboarders from their streets and other public places. Soon the skate parks were forced to close. By the early 1980s they had virtually disappeared.

Skate parks return

By the mid-1980s, local councils began to change their laws against skateboarding in public places. This made it possible for skate parks to operate. Before long, more skate parks began to open across the United States, dotting the country from east to west. Cities and towns throughout much of the Western world followed their lead.

Skate parks and public skating areas can now be found in most communities, from the United States to the United Kingdom, Australia and Japan.

BMX racing takes place on tracks such as these, or on trails sculpted with jumps and obstacles.

Dirt tracks for BMX

Many local communities provide excellent dirt tracks for BMX racing. These tracks resemble miniature motocross circuits. They provide an excellent venue to learn the sport, since many BMX clubs provide coaching and age-level competitions.

BMX trails are also popular. They are usually found on vacant blocks of land, and consist of a number of dirt jumps and assorted obstacles placed in a challenging circuit layout. BMX trails are often sculpted by the riders themselves. The trails continually evolve as new features are added.

No skating in public places

It is hazardous to skate in busy public places such as carparks and shopping malls. In order to restrict skating in these places, signs are posted forbidding the use of skateboards. Usually there is an appropriate venue nearby.

Multi-purpose venues

When inline skates first came onto the market in the 1980s, they were mainly used on the streets and sidewalks by fitness fanatics and athletes in training for other sports. From about the middle of that decade and into the early 1990s, inline skating in skate parks became popular. At the same time, BMX riders discovered that skate parks were well suited to performing tricks on their bikes. Today, followers of all three street sports can be found at these multi-purpose venues.

Closed roads

Street luge also originated in southern California, in the United States. Street luge races are held on steep winding roads. Local authorities usually close off the road to vehicles for an event. In some parts of the United States, however, lugers have to practice on roads that may also contain light traffic. Away from town, access roads to ski resorts and closed mountain roads make ideal street luge venues.

Gear Up for the Streets

EXTREME SPORTS PROMOTE PRODUCTS

Many extreme sports are closely associated with youth culture. Extreme sports are often featured in advertising campaigns. Street sports such as skateboarding and aggressive inline skating are used to promote products ranging from food and soft drinks to clothing and footwear. People are often attracted to these products because they like the extreme sports image.

WEAR LOOSE-FITTING CLOTHES

The clothing most often associated with the skating culture generally consists of a loose-fitting sweatshirt or T-shirt, and baggy shorts or cargo pants. T-shirts and sweatshirts often feature the logo and brand name of a company closely associated with the sport. The loose fit helps the skater perform tricks that require great flexibility and body movement. A backwards-pointing baseball cap usually completes the 'look'.

CHOOSE SHOES THAT CUSHION

Many skateboarders wear lightweight shoes designed especially for the sport. Shoes suffer lots of wear and tear through constant contact with concrete and asphalt. Skateboarding shoes need to be abrasion resistant and durable. They have to withstand harsh treatment. Shoes must also provide protection for the feet. Shoes that feature rubber toecaps, cushioned soles and shock-absorbing heels will help reduce the heavy impact of landings.

MINIMIZE THE RISKS

Aggressive inline skaters wear similar loose clothing. This also reflects their skating culture. When performing tricks in a skate park, there is always the danger of serious injury from an awkward landing on the concrete. Wearing protective knee and elbow pads and a helmet minimizes the risk.

Wearing protective padding will minimize the risk of injury.

helmet

wrist pads

elbow pads

kneepads

inline skates

BMX racing often involves collisions and spills, so riders tend to opt for full body protection.

helmet

long-sleeved racing top with extra padding

gloves

kneepads

protective shoes

Use added protection when racing

BMX racing is often regarded as a **contact sport**. There are frequent collisions when racers go into the tight corners of a dirt course. BMX racers generally prefer to wear long-sleeved racing tops with extra padding. The long sleeves provide added protection to the skin on the arms in the event of a spill or fall.

Xtreme Fact
Many street sports clothing companies sponsor professional teams. Their athletes tour, compete, coach and give demonstrations while promoting the sponsors' products.

BE PREPARED ON THE LUGE

Street lugers reach speeds in excess of 100 kilometers (62 miles) per hour while their bodies are extended just inches above the road surface. In the event of a crash or a fall at that speed, the risk of serious injury is very high. In order to protect the skin from accidental contact with the road surface, lugers wear full-body leathers, similar to those worn by elite motorcycle racers. Leather gloves protect their hands, and a full-face helmet guards against head injury.

AVOID INJURY ON THE BMX

BMX riders prefer loose-fitting clothes. This provides the ease of movement required for performing tricks on the bikes. A collision or a fall from a bike could result in serious injury, so gloves, a helmet, knee pads and elbow pads are essential.

Use shoes as brakes

Street lugers use their feet as brakes at the bottom of a hill. This places their shoes under a great deal of stress. Lugers' shoes need to have soles that are capable of gripping the road surface and are able to withstand plenty of wear and tear. Many lugers modify their shoes by securely fixing strips of rubber from a car tire to each of the soles.

Safety on the Streets

Be properly trained

When the world's best skateboarders and aggressive inline skaters perform demonstrations or compete in televised events, their feats are considered to be outstanding. Spectators are treated to incredible displays of aerial acrobatics on wheels as the athletes spin and twist above the ground. They make it look easy.

Misguided onlookers sometimes fancy themselves performing similar antics. It is unwise to try these sports without proper training and practice. Street sports often take years to master. Almost daily practice is required to perform well at the levels displayed in exhibitions and competitions.

Street sports often take years to master. Learn the simple tricks first.

Build a railslide

One way to learn to **slide and grind** on a skateboard without taking too many unnecessary risks is to build yourself a railslide. In its simplest form, a rail slide is little more than a length of steel pipe (approximately 2 meters (6.6 feet) long and 5 centimeters (2 inches) in diameter), similar to that used in a handrail on stairs, securely attached to a solid base. The base could be approximately 2 meters long, 20 centimeters (7.8 inches) wide and 15 centimeters (6 inches) high. Mount the pipe parallel to and a few inches above the base. Now you can practice your slides and grinds in your own backyard or driveway while remaining relatively close to the safety of the ground.

Learn simple tricks first

Find simple ways to learn the skills and tricks of street sports in safety before attempting them in a public place such as a skate park. Practice getting the simplest skills under control first. Gradually increase the level of difficulty until you have gained the ability to perform more complex tricks both confidently and competently.

Respect your fear

Even the world's best skaters understand and respect the fear produced when participating in extreme sports. It keeps them on their toes, ever alert for the slightest irregularity that could cause a nasty spill. Learning to respect and control fear is one of the factors that helps skaters all the way to the top of their sport.

Skateboards and BMX bikes are built to withstand rough treatment, but they should still be serviced regularly.

Guard against hazards

All participants in extreme sports need to be aware of the potential risks that confront them. If there is a risk of serious injury to any part of the body, the appropriate protection should be worn. Helmets are not always necessary for skateboarding or inline skating, but if the intention is to perform dangerous stunts, it is advisable to wear them. Suitable padding is important when there is an element of risk that involves the knees and elbows.

Keep your gear in good condition

It is vital to keep all equipment in good working order. For example, the presence of dirt and grit particles in the **bearings** on a street luge can cause enough friction to melt the bearing where it makes contact with the wheel. This can cause the wheels to stop turning altogether. The result may be a terrible accident at high speed.

Xtreme Fact

In 1993, more than 31,000 people in the United States visited emergency medical centers with inline-skating injuries. By far, the most common injuries suffered were to the wrists.

Maintain your equipment

The manufacturers of skateboards, inline skates, BMX bikes and street luges build their products to withstand punishing treatment. However, in order to get the best performance from the gear, they should be serviced regularly. Keep all moving parts free of obstruction.

THE FIRST SKATEBOARDS

The first skateboards were little more than boards attached to sets of rollerskate wheels. They were fun to ride on the pavement, but there was little more you could do with them. A couple of improvements to their basic design in the early 1970s changed all of that. A tail was added to the **deck**, allowing the rider to maneuver the board easily. Polyurethane wheels were invented, providing increased traction and speed.

Different skateboards suit different styles of riding.

Skateboard design

The basic elements of a skateboard are:

- ☞ a wooden deck which the rider stands on
- ☞ front and rear sets of steering and axle assemblies, known as trucks
- ☞ two wheels attached to each set of trucks.

Different boards for different styles

Skateboard designs soon evolved to suit different styles of riding. Some boards combined longer decks with wider trucks. This allowed for stable street cruising at high speeds. Shorter, lighter boards made it easier for stunt riders to perform tricks. For several years, all forms of skateboarding were popular.

Skateboarding takes a tumble

By the end of the 1970s, public interest in skateboarding had declined. Most existing skate parks closed down. Not everyone abandoned the sport, however. A small number of skaters turned their energy to creating their own wooden skate parks on vacant blocks of land. By 1982, they were holding their own skating competitions.

A skateboarding revival

In 1984, a skateboarding video featuring spectacular action footage was released. The video, produced by George Powell and Stacy Peralta, was called *The Bones Brigade Video Show*, and featured some of the biggest names in skateboarding. It generated a great deal of interest, and it was not long before skateboards were popular once again.

SKATEBOARDING

Xtreme Fact

Skateboarding legend Andy Macdonald broke his own world record in gap jumping at Lake Havasu, Arizona in March 2000. He cleared more than 17.3 meters (57 feet).

two wheels attached to each set of trucks

front trucks

wooden deck

rear trucks

Snowboarding

On the ski slopes, snowboarding offered people the opportunity to have a great time without using traditional skis. Despite their lack of wheels, snowboards behaved in a similar way to skateboards. They were ideal for carving big turns. Spectacular stunts could be performed with them in the **halfpipe**. Many skateboarders found they were equally at home performing tricks on the snowboard. Snowboarding became a perfect winter diversion for many skateboarders.

Wakeboarding

In the water, wakeboarders developed their new sport around skateboarding principles. Wakeboarding features many of the spectacular jumps and re-entries that skateboarders perform in skate parks.

Inline skating and street luge

Skateboarding has had a huge influence on the development of other street sports. Street luge originated when skateboarders began to lie down on their boards. The inline skating culture is quite similar to that of skateboarding. Enthusiasts of both sports share very similar interests in lifestyle, clothing and music. Both sports feature similar stunts in skate parks and on the streets.

Setting new trends

By the mid-1990s, skateboarding was well established throughout the world, particularly in the youth cultures of Western countries. It gained huge television exposure during the first Extreme Games, held in the United States in 1995. Many athletes from other sports began to take up skateboarding as a valuable cross-training activity. It was around this time that skateboarding began to exert a strong influence on the development of new sports.

Gap jumping is one of the daredevil stunts performed by street style skaters.

Two types of skateboarding

There are basically two types of skateboarding today, **street style** and **vert style**. Both styles challenge skaters to perform bigger and better tricks in the quest for an **adrenaline rush**

Street style

Street skaters take their craft to the public places around their cities. They can be found on sidewalks, in parks, industrial estates, on city squares and spacious courtyards. Wherever there are flights of stairs, handrails, benches and expanses of concrete on several levels, street skaters are likely to congregate. Street skating is considered to be perhaps the most difficult form of the sport to master. Street tricks look spectacular when performed, but often take years to learn.

HANDRAIL SLIDE

A session in a city park may begin with a **noseslide** down the handrail of a flight of 15 stairs. In order to do this, you must first **ollie** and land on the nose of your board at the top of the rail. Then, with your arms and legs spread to maintain your balance, ride the board on its nose all the way to the bottom of the stairs, **take air** again at the bottom, and land smoothly to continue the ride.

DAREDEVIL GAP JUMPING

From the noseslide you might move from one obstacle to the next, executing a series of gravity defying stunts. These might involve many **variations** of slides, grinds, jumps, spins and flips. Gap jumping, where you take off from one obstacle and land several feet away on another, is a stunt that many street skaters enjoy.

Street Skating and Vert Skating

Brian Patch takes air on the halfpipe during the 1998 Summer X Games, held in Queensland.

Xtreme Fact

Tony Hawk became a professional skateboarder at the age of 14. Since then he has won numerous world titles. He was the first skater to perform several tricks in competition, including the 540 kickflip.

Vert style

Vert skating usually takes place in a halfpipe. The halfpipe is a U-shaped ramp with two vertical walls connected by rounded surfaces called transitions. The transitions take you down one vertical surface, across a horizontal surface, and up the vertical surface on the opposing side wall. A typical competition halfpipe is about 9.75 meters (32 feet) wide, and each vert wall is about 3.2 meters (10.5 feet) high.

THE COPING

The slightly protruding concrete edge or steel pipe that lies along the top edge of each vert wall is the coping. The coping acts as the surface along which you can perform vert tricks such as sliding or grinding. Its presence also lets you know that you have crossed the top of the wall. It even helps you retain control of your board in the air, by deflecting the board back towards you as it leaves the top of the ramp.

AERIAL STUNTS

Many breathtaking tricks are performed in the air, high above the halfpipe. At the Summer X Games in 1999, skateboarding legend Tony Hawk completed the first '900' ever performed in vert skating competition history. He turned his body through 900 degrees, or 2.5 rotations in the air, before landing to rapturous applause from the spectators.

SUMMER X GAMES ACTION

The Summer X Games showcases the top performers in both street and vert skating. There are usually world-class displays in both disciplines. Street skaters are allowed two 60-second runs to perform their stunts, while vert skaters have two 50-second runs. They score points for consistency, style and the degree of difficulty of their tricks.

Learn to ollie

The ollie is probably the first trick to learn. It takes its name from its inventor, Ollie Gelfand. Use the ollie to take air or to jump your board. You can also use it to begin other tricks by jumping your board from the ground onto an obstacle. For example, you might ollie onto a bench or a handrail to begin a grind or a slide. At high speeds, the ollie is a reliable way of travelling over unpredictable terrain.

The ollie is performed by standing with your back foot on the tail of the board, while your front foot is placed on the center of the board. Jump up, and the board comes up with your feet. Slide your front foot forward until your board levels out. Land the board with one foot over each set of trucks. For variation, start with a nollie by tapping the nose of the board, rather than the tail, to begin the jump.

Try the kickflip

Another popular trick is the kickflip. As you begin to ollie, kick one foot down on the outside of your board. This will cause your board to spin through a complete rotation before your front foot comes down to steady the board for landing.

New tricks and variations

New tricks are constantly evolving as skateboarders continue to push their skills to the limits. Even well-established tricks are developing into new variations. Each trick is identified by a unique name. Some tricks are named after their creators, while others take their names from the special features of the trick itself.

Skateboarding Tricks

Vary your slide

Most skaters enjoy sliding and grinding. You can create variations of each of these stunts by using different parts of your board to perform the trick. Sliding involves using the underside of the deck to move along the coping or the top of an obstacle. Slide variations include the railslide, where you use the underside between the trucks to perform the trick. Others include the noseslide and tailslide, where you use either end of the board.

Master the grind

To grind, move along the coping of an obstacle while riding on your board's axles. You can vary your grinding by changing your stance, or by restricting the grind to either the front or rear axle.

Use your hands

Skaters often use their hands to perform tricks. Grabs and handplants are examples of such tricks. There are many variations of grabs, in which you grasp the board in different places while taking air. To perform a handplant, do a one-handed handstand on the coping while holding your board high in the air with your other hand or your feet.

Perform the Caballerial and the McTwist

A couple of tricks named after their inventors are the Caballerial and the McTwist. The Caballerial was named after Steve Caballero. To perform it, ride **fakie** up the transition, hit the coping and spin through 360 degrees in the air before heading forwards down the ramp. Mike McGill invented the McTwist, which involves a 540-degree turn off a ramp, in the opposite direction to that which you are facing.

Xtreme Fact

When champion skateboarder Andy Macdonald visited Australia in 1999, he performed at 56 different skate parks over just 19 days. Doing lots of stretching exercises keeps him in shape for skating.

HOW AGGRESSIVE INLINE SKATING STARTED

The sport of aggressive inline skating can probably trace its birth to 1979, when Scott and Brennan Olsen bought some inexpensive inline skates. They decided to make a couple of design improvements, in the hope that the skates would be useful for off-season ice hockey training. The brothers removed the flimsy wheels and replaced them with polyurethane ones. They also added a rubber heel brake for stability.

Rollerblades hit the market

Scott Olsen started up a company to produce the improved inline skates, which he called Rollerblades. Each skate consisted of an inline chassis attached to an ice hockey boot. Within a few years, Olsen sold the company, and the new owners soon produced an improved model.

Cross-training for skiers

By the mid-1980s, people had discovered that Rollerblading on a pavement could provide a carving sensation, somewhat similar to the action of skis on snow. This opened up a huge new market. Many skiers took up inline skating as a summer cross-training activity.

Skating for fitness

Fitness fanatics also took to inline skating as a fun alternative to jogging. By the end of the 1980s, inline skating was well established in the United States and in other countries. People found it a fun way to get around and stay fit at the same time.

New ways to use the skates

At around this time, a new generation of inline skaters, heavily influenced by skateboarding, began looking for more exciting ways to use the skates. They ventured to the same skate parks and public places as the boarders. There they found that street style and vert style tricks were just as well suited to their inline skates.

The frontside is one of the first grinds to learn.

Xtreme Fact

The first inline skate was probably invented by Robert John Tyers of London, in 1823. He made a 'rolito' by adding five wheels in line to the bottom of a shoe. Unfortunately, it did not work.

Inline skating at skate parks

When inline skaters first appeared in skate parks, they were not always made welcome by skateboarders. The best way to win the confidence of the skateboarding community was to perform to the same high standards that they did, and this is what inline skaters set about to do. It did not take long before the new breed of skaters were performing breathtaking stunts that equalled anything the board riders could offer. Both groups soon developed a healthy respect for each others' skills, and most of the tensions eased. Today, you can find enthusiasts of both sports happily 'strutting their stuff', side by side, at most skate parks.

Halfpipe acrobatics

Many inline skaters have developed their sport to a fine art on the halfpipe. They use it to launch themselves high into the air above the coping, where they spin and twist their bodies through an amazing array of tricks.

Some inline skaters spend many hours practicing acrobatic stunts on the halfpipe.

Inline tricks

Many vert inline skating tricks originated directly from skateboarding tricks of the same names. They are performed in a similar way, and require much the same skills. Inline skaters perform their own variations of airs, flips, turns, grabs, handplants and grinds.

Feet movements

Perhaps the biggest difference between the ways the tricks are performed relates to the differences in the equipment. An inline skater's feet are free to move independently of each other, while a skateboarder's feet are used to retain control of the board through the air.

The 360 spin is one of the basic tricks performed by aggressive inline skaters.

A fun sport

Aggressive inline skating is a fun sport. Many skaters enjoy a session of street style skating in a park or other public place brimming with stairs, rails, benches, curbs and other obstacles. There are many excellent tricks that feature in this version of the sport, and countless variations on those.

The 360 spin

Perhaps one of the more basic street tricks is the '360', a stunt in which the skater takes air and spins through a complete circle before landing. To begin a 360, approach your take-off point in a crouch position, with both arms to one side. As you spring into the air, swing both arms hard around to the other side of your body to begin the spin, then pull back in to form a tight body shape. Look over one shoulder to a landing point, and remain focused on it as your body unwinds and lands.

Variations on the 360

There are a number of variations of this trick, although some are quite a bit harder to learn and perform. The '540' involves one and a half complete turns. The '720' is two complete turns. Obviously, the better you are at taking air, the easier these tricks become. You can also perform fakie on each of these tricks.

Grinding

In order to grind across obstacles, inline skates have special grind plates attached to the **chassis**, between the front two wheels and the back two wheels. These prevent any accidental damage to the chassis from grinding, and also stop the wheels from 'grabbing' the obstacle.

Grind variations

A few interesting grind variations are the frontside grind, soul grind and miszou grind. The frontside is one of the first grinds to learn. Turn your body to face the obstacle, then grind down the obstacle, with your skates almost at right angles to the direction of the grind.

Xtreme Fact

In the official Aggressive Skaters Association street skating scoring system, competitors are scored on a possible total of 80 points. For every competitor, each of the seven judges scores points out of 30 for airs, 30 for grinds and 20 for use of the apparatus. The highest and lowest scores are dropped, and the rest is tallied for a score out of 400.

SOUL GRIND

The soul grind is a slower grind than the frontside. To perform this trick, place your front foot perpendicular to the rail, similar to the frontside, but with your back foot parallel to the rail. Slide your front foot on the grind plate, but grind the back on the soul, which is the bottom of the boot next to the wheels. Place your weight on the soul foot, which does the grinding in this trick.

MISZOU GRIND

The miszou grind is a variation on the soul grind. Make your front foot the soul foot, and place it parallel to the obstacle. This foot takes your weight. Turn your back foot at right angles to the obstacle, and slide on the grind plate between the second and third wheels.

Misty flip

This is a great trick performed by experienced skaters. You turn a forward somersault while bringing your knees up to your chin and twisting through 540 degrees. You will need full protection from helmet and padding to perform these tricks. The safest way to learn the misty flip is to practice from the diving board of a swimming pool.

BMX RIDING

EXTREME BIKE RIDING

BMX stands for 'Bicycle Motocross'. It takes its name from motocross, which is an extreme sport for off-road motorbikes. BMX riding offers a number of different formats, and each has its own group of dedicated fans. The BMX formats include:

- ☛ BMX racing
- ☛ vert style
- ☛ street style
- ☛ dirt riding
- ☛ flatland riding.

A bike for tough conditions

BMX bikes are much smaller than mountain bikes. Their wheels are generally about 50 centimeters (19.5 inches) in diameter. Smaller-style bikes came onto the market during the 1960s. Riders discovered that their smaller wheels and fatter tires made them much easier to maneuver than larger bikes, particularly on dirt surfaces. BMX bikes soon became popular when riders found the bikes could withstand plenty of punishing treatment.

Dirt track racing

In the early 1970s, a group of Californian teenagers began to set up their own BMX races. They fashioned a dirt track on a vacant block to resemble a miniature motocross track. The track included sharp corners, obstacles and dirt mounds for jumping.

The sport grows

Throughout the 1970s, the popularity of BMX racing spread throughout the United States and around the world. Clubs catered for all ages, and held regular weekend events. As the sport grew, the bikes and the riders got better and better. Some were capable of reaching speeds in excess of 100 kilometers (62 miles) per hour on tricky dirt courses.

BMX goes to Hollywood

When Steven Spielberg's hit movie *E.T.* was released in 1982, BMX bike sales received a boost. The bikes played a prominent role in some of the movie's most memorable scenes.

BMX racing is one of the many different forms of BMX riding.

The size of the BMX bike allows riders to perform spectacular stunts, such as rotating while taking air.

grind pegs

GLOSSARY

freestyle – a form of the BMX sport where tricks are performed

Street style or vert style?

The new stunt bikes led to the development of a range of street style tricks. Skateboarders soon found themselves sharing the concrete ramps and assorted obstacles of local parks and other public places with the new generation of BMX riders. Some bikers discovered the gravity defying thrills of halfpipe tricks, and adapted their bikes to vert style riding. BMX riders became another group which frequented the skate parks.

Grind pegs

Stunt riders attach a simple piece of equipment to their bikes. A small metal tube called a 'grind peg' is attached to each side of both the front and rear axles. This gives the rider the ability to grind the bike along the coping and other obstacles.

Aerial stunts

When they are not grinding along the top edge of the halfpipe, vert riders perform most of their tricks high above the coping. As the bike leaves the transition and soars upwards of 3 meters (10 feet) into the air, the rider grabs the handlebars and spins through one or more complete rotations before re-entering the halfpipe and riding out the trick.

Avoiding injury

Such daredevil riding requires both street and vert bikers to wear helmets and full padding. A fall while performing a stunt could easily result in serious injury.

A bike especially for tricks

In the early 1980s, some BMX riders began practicing tricks with their bikes. They found that the bikes were great for taking air off the dirt jumps. The interest in stunt, or **freestyle**, riding grew. By 1983, the Mongoose company designed a specialized frame, and released the world's first commercial freestyle BMX bike.

BMX Events

Racing

There are many official events available for BMX bikers, and each varies considerably from the others. BMX racing is still popular. Up to eight riders compete in each heat, which is known as a 'moto'. A moto is one circuit of the dirt track. Riders burst out of the gates and navigate a series of tight corners, jumps and other obstacles on their way to the finish line. It gets crowded on the turns, so they have to use great skill to avoid collisions on their way around. In order to reach the final, riders must make it through three elimination motos.

Dirt events

Dirt events evolved from BMX racing. These events involve taking big air from dirt jumps and performing variations of different tricks while airborne. The higher you can go over the jump, the more opportunity there is to execute a winning stunt before landing smoothly several feet away, on another dirt ramp. A particularly challenging event is the triple jump, where you are confronted by three bone-jarring jumps in succession, just 4 or 5 meters (13 to 16 feet) apart.

Street style competitions

Street competitions usually consist of a number of different types and styles of ramp. The ramps are positioned around the edges of the area within which you must perform. A quarterpipe, which resembles a single wall of a halfpipe, often features in a street competition layout. Using the various ramps, street competitors must perform a routine which displays a variety of skills and tricks such as taking air, grinding, spinning and twisting.

This competitor is performing the second of six sequences in the dirt jump competition at the 1998 Summer X Games, held on the Gold Coast, Queensland.

Vert style events

The BMX vert event is held in a halfpipe. You enter the halfpipe from one platform and build speed as you pedal down one transition, across the horizontal plane and up the other side. The faster you are going when you reach the coping on the far wall, the higher you will soar. Judges rate you on the quality of your aerial tricks, as well as on those you perform on the coping.

Vert doubles competition

A spectacular variation of the vert style event is the vert doubles competition. In this event, two riders work the halfpipe at the same time. Spectators are treated to dual aerial displays as the two riders leave the coping at the same time.

Flatland events

Another BMX event is flatland. You have to perform tricks by stepping over and around your bike while it keeps moving on a flat surface, usually asphalt or concrete. You use the grind pegs protruding from the front and rear axles as foot pegs to stand on while you spin around your bike beneath you, and perform other amazing balancing feats.

Your feet must not touch the ground, and all moves must take place in a continuous, fluid motion. Judges award points for originality and style, as well as for the degree of difficulty of each move and the way you link each move to the next. It takes years and years of practice to become a top flatland rider.

Summer X Games action

BMX events are a highlight of the annual Summer X Games. Medals are awarded for dirt, vert, street and flatland competitions. The Summer X Games began in 1995, when the American ESPN television network decided to bring the world's best extreme athletes together for a series of explosive events.

Xtreme Fact

Matt Hoffman won the vert world title eight years in a row. He also set a world record of over 15 meters (49 feet) for a vertical jump, but ruptured his spleen on landing.

Flatland riders perform tricks by stepping over and around their moving bikes.

A NEW STREET SPORT

Luge is an event that always attracts plenty of interest at the Winter Olympic Games. Competitors hurtle down winding, icy chutes in sleds that rely only on gravity and subtle shifts of the body to get the competitors safely over the finish line. Similar techniques, combined with motor racing design and engineering, are used in the relatively new sport of street luge.

ying down on a skateboard

Street luge started when skateboarders lay down on their boards at the top of a steep winding road and raced each other down the slope. It is claimed that Bob Pereyra of the United States, one of the pioneers of the sport, once ran out of gas while travelling in a mountain area. The legend says that he pulled his skateboard out of the car, lay down on it and rode it down the mountain road.

PEREYRA'S PLACE IN STREET LUGE HISTORY

The accuracy of this story cannot be guaranteed, but Pereyra will surely retain a special place in the history of street luge. He was the first person to set down the rules of the new sport, and to organize the first official street luge competitions. Pereyra also founded the Roadracers Association for International Luge, in 1990. He once won an X Games gold medal while nursing a broken foot he had suffered during a preliminary heat.

Custom-made sleds

The first street lugers built their own sleds. As the sport developed, manufacturers began to produce luges that were technologically quite advanced. Today, each professional rider's sled is custom built to fit their body size and shape. A strong, lightweight aluminum chassis is mounted on similar trucks to those used on skateboards.

Each professional street luger's sled is custom built to fit their body size and shape. The first street lugers built their own sleds.

STREET LUGE

BUILT FOR SPEED

In a street luge competition you lie flat on your back, in a molded seat pan that is lowered to suit your body's contour. This part of the luge is usually only a fraction of an inch above the road surface. The handlebars at the front end of the seat pan are located on the side of each hip. This helps you to remain aboard the luge, and lean to steer it.

SAFETY DESIGN FEATURE

Your head rests on a slightly raised headrest, just forward of the rear trucks. The front trucks are beneath your thighs. At the front end of the luge are short foot pegs. Rounded bars, called 'nerf bars', join the outer ends of the pegs to the front of the chassis. This helps to ensure that you are not accidentally hooked during a race by the foot pegs of other competitors' luges.

LEAN-ACTIVATED STEERING

The urethane wheels of a luge are suspended on trucks activated when you lean in the direction you want to go. When you lean to the right, the pressure on the right-side wheels steers the luge in that direction, and vice versa. If there is any grit in the wheel bearings causing friction, the heat generated at speeds in excess of 110 kilometers (68 miles) per hour can destroy the wheel in an instant. You need to take extreme caution with the condition of the wheels and bearings.

Full body protection

The dangers of travelling downhill at high speed in such an open vehicle are obvious, especially considering that your head and limbs are positioned so close to the road surface. It is essential that you wear a full-face helmet, a padded leather racing suit, leather gloves and thick-soled shoes.

The street luge is built for speed.

rear trucks

head rest

handlebars at the seat pan

foot pegs

nerf bars

Xtreme Fact
Bumpers made of rubber or another suitable material must be attached to the front and rear of each competition luge.

Three racing formats

There are three different race formats for street luge. These are timed, dual and mass races. Timed events pit the racers against the clock, with only one racer on the course at a time. A luge pilot in California was timed at just over 135 kilometers (84 miles) per hour! This makes street luge one of the world's fastest non-motorized sports.

Battling the dual event

In dual events, two lugers battle each other down the course, head-to-head in a race of tactics and speed. Mass luge races usually feature four, six or even eight pilots, depending on the limitations of the course. Both dual and mass events receive broad television coverage through their inclusion in the annual Summer X Games.

Taking to the course

Races are often held close to cities on closed, winding hilly roads. Further away from town, events can take place on closed mountain roads, or on ski resort access roads during the skiing off-season. The lengths of courses vary from a couple of miles to over ten. Before an event the roads are often carefully cleared of stones and other potentially hazardous objects.

Starting

The lugers line up side by side behind the starting line. All pilots must be sitting upright. When the start signal is given, you propel yourself forward by paddling with your hands. Once you are beyond a restricted push-off zone, gravity takes over. You need great upper-arm strength for paddling.

Riding

For the remainder of the race, you must lie straight, with your toes pointed, arms by your sides and your head down to minimize wind resistance. You have to raise your head slightly and peer between your toes to see where you are heading.

The mass luge race at the 1998 X Games, held in Brisbane.

Street Luge Racing

GLOSSARY

slipstream – the air current behind a moving object

Xtreme Fact

Any luge pilot who does not have all safety gear still in place at the finish of a race is automatically disqualified.

Lugers use the slipstream behind the lead racer to overtake.

Avoiding collisions

When two luge pilots approach a corner together, one often has to back off a little and let the other through first, or risk an horrific collision. Collisions also occur when one luger pulls into another's slipstream, accelerates and clips the leading racer on a poorly executed overtaking move. Each luger must ensure that they are fully under control before moving out to overtake other racers. High-speed collisions can result in serious injuries.

Taking corners

You steer by leaning, or by just slightly turning your shoulders when entering a bend. On sharp corners, you may have to drag your feet and sit a little more upright to create greater wind resistance. The combination of these two actions will slow you down enough to take the corners under control. Hay bales are generally placed on sharp bends, to protect lugers who fail to take the corners.

Stopping without brakes

At the finish of the course, lugers drag their feet on the road surface to stop. Hay bales are placed behind the finish line to protect racers and spectators in the event of a mishap. Managing to stand to their feet as the sled comes to a halt provides a crowd-pleasing finish to an exhilarating race.

Using the slipstream

One tactic you might use is to tuck into the **slipstream**, close behind the lead racer. If you are behind the lead racer, this places you in an area of less wind resistance. You can use this lack of wind resistance just long enough to accelerate and pass the leader.

Street Jargon

bust a jib
to successfully complete a difficult trick

"I've been trying to bust that jib for weeks now."

freaking out
to be scared

"I was freaking out as I left the coping and took huge air."

gnarly
awesome; really challenging

"The local skate park has a gnarly new vert ramp."

grommet
an adolescent skater

"There were a couple of grommets rail sliding down at the park."

huck
to recklessly launch off the coping in a quest for big air

"I watched him huck a couple of huge nollie heelflips."

jamming
getting together with your friends for a skating session

"A few of us buds were jamming down at the skate park."

pad up
put on protective padding

"She had to pad up well before going vertical off the halfpipe."

phat
a reference to either the distance or the height of a skating trick (pronounced 'fat')

"I went really phat off the handrail."

rad
excellent; fun (short for 'radical')

"We had a rad session on the halfpipe."

stack
a collision or crash

"I was nursing a bruised shoulder from a big stack."

stoked
really fired up; enthusiastic

"The crowd was really stoked as they watched him successfully land a big 540."

tech
complex skating involving flipping and other freestyle tricks

"He scored serious points with a couple of tech moves."

Glossary

adrenaline rush
the special feeling that accompanies a thrilling event

bearings
the small metal balls inside the wheels which bear the friction

chassis
the frame and wheel assembly of an inline skate or street luge

contact sport
any sport which involves body-to-body contact with a competitor

deck
the platform area of a skateboard

fakie
skating backwards

freestyle
a form of the BMX sport where tricks are performed

halfpipe
a U-shaped ramp with two vert walls joined by transitions, usually found in a skate park

noseslide
to slide along the coping or a rail on the nose, or in front, of the skateboard

ollie
to take air without using the hands; a common trick used in skateboarding and aggressive inline skating

skate park
a community area featuring a halfpipe, bowls, ramps and other obstacles used by street sports enthusiasts

slide and grind
to slide along the edge of an obstacle

slipstream
the air current behind a moving object

street style
a style of skateboarding which features tricks performed on obstacles found in public places, such as benches, stairs and rails

take air
a jump or leap

transitions
the curved walls that join the horizontal plane to the vert wall on a ramp or halfpipe

tricks
also known as stunts; the movements performed in street sports that include airs, grinds, slides, grabs, spins and flips

trucks
the axle systems that connect the wheels to the deck of a skateboard

variations
changes made to tricks to create entirely new tricks

vert style
a style of skateboarding which features tricks performed on and above the coping at the top edge of the vertical wall of a halfpipe

Index